Introduction

The Mahatma Gandhi National Rural Employment Guarantee Scheme (MGNREGS), a labour intensive public works program. In the first phase was, the scheme was implemented in 200 most backward districts of the country from February 2006. In April 2007, an additional 130 districts were included under phase II, bringing the total districts under it to 330 districts. From April 2008, under phase III, MGNREGS has been extended to all 644 rural districts in the country to guarantee at least 100 days of wage employment to every rural household every year and to reinforce the commitment towards livelihood security in rural areas. The program also envisages protecting environment, reducing migration, financial inclusion besides empowerment of rural women and creation of sustainable rural assets.

This chapter focuses on the performance of the scheme at national, state level and sample district level. The performance evaluation has been done on the basis of secondary data extracted from MGNREGS web portal and state websites. Besides, the implementation mechanism of MGNREGS has also been evaluated to understand the effectiveness and challenges involved in its implementation. This was done by collecting information from the functionaries involved in the implementation of MGNREGS. It is eventually the proper implementation not the mere introduction of a scheme which determines its success or failure in the long run.

Performance of MGNREGS at National Level

The performance of MGNREGS has been dismal as can be seen from its physical and financial performance over a period of time. The major problems are under utilization of budgetary resources, poor execution of works, employment rate has been declining, poor rate of average man-days generated etc. All of these problems point towards one major fact which is poor implementation of the scheme at national level.

The table below depicts the physical and financial performance of the scheme over a period beginning 2008-09 to financial year 2014-15. It is quite evident from the table that a significant amount of budget outlay has been allocated to MGNREGS over a period of time. The budget outlay for FY 2013-14 was Rs 33,000 crore and the expenditure for the same year has been Rs 24,848 crore. Therefore, the problem is that a substantial proportion of budget outlay for the scheme has remained unspent in almost every year. This reflects the inefficiency in making use of the budget outlay in a stipulated time, thereby defeating the very purpose of this largest workfare scheme in the world.

A careful look at the table below reveals that there has been a decline in the number of rural households' who have been provided employment in MGNREGS scheme. In 2008-09, 4.5 crore households' got employment, which increased to a high of 5.5 crore in 2010-11 and then declined to 4.13 crore in 2014-15 *(www.nrega.nic.in)*.

The man-days generated reveals that in 2014-15 only 40 Average-Man Days were generated which is starkly lower than that of 54 Average-Man Days generated in 2009-10. These statistics regarding Man-days generated in MGNREGS for the reference period reflect that the guaranteed 100 days target has never been achieved. This reveals the poor management and implementation of the scheme at national level. In FY 2013-14, a mammoth 111.6 lakh works were selected for execution out of which just 11.17 lakh got completed, a staggering deficit of 100 lakh. This yet again reflects on the poor management and execution skills of the implementing agencies at all levels.

Table 1: Performance of MGNREGS at National Level

Performance	FY 2008-09	FY 2009-10	FY 2010-11	FY 2011-12	FY 2012-13	FY 2013-14	FY 2014-15
No. of Households Employed (Crore)	4.5	5.3	5.5	5	4.98	4.79	4.13
Total	216.3	283.6	257.2	209.3	229.86	220.37	166.21
SCs	63.4 (29%)	86.5 (30%)	78.8 (31%)	46.2 (22%)	50.96 (22%)	31.53 (22.81%)	37.23 (22.4%)

STs	55 (25%)	58.7 (21%)	53.6 (21%)	37.7 (18%)	40.75 (18%)	21.09 (17.52%)	28.20 (16.97%)
Women	103.6 (48%)	136.4 (48%)	122.7 (48%)	101.11 (48%)	117.93 (51%)	73.33 (52.82%)	91.21 (54.88%)
Average person-days per (HH)	48 days	54 days	47 days	47 days	46 days	46 days	40 days
Expenditure (Rs crores)	27250	37905	39377	37303	39262	24848	24800
Works Taken Up	27.8	46.2	51	73.6	106.51	111.6	98
Works Completed	12.1	22.6	25.9	14.3	26.60	11.17	29.44

Source: www.nrega.nic.in

Profile of the Study Area

Figure 1: Map Showing Jammu & Kashmir and Various Districts

Source: www.mapsofindia.com

The State of Jammu and Kashmir strategically speaking is a prominent State in the Indian Union. The state of Jammu and Kashmir which is located in hilly terrain having an area of 2630 sq. KMs.between 70°-0° to 74°-40° east longitude and 32°-58° to 33°-35° north latitude. The State comprises three divisions namely, Jammu, Kashmir and Ladakh. And, for administrative purposes, it has been demarcated into two divisions, i.e., Kashmir and Jammu spread over twelve and ten districts, respectively including the eight districts which have recently been carved out from the existing districts. There are 121 Community Development Blocks, 2,661 Panchayats and 6652 villages. The study was conducted in Kupwara and Poonch districts of J&K state.

The economy of the state of J&K is dominated by agriculture with 70% of population deriving their livelihood from the sector. The Gross State Domestic Product at constant (2004-05) prices for the year 2014-15 is estimated at Rs. 45126.30 crores (Advance Estimates) as against Rs. 45847.15 crores for the year 2013-14 (1st Revised Estimates) registering a negative growth of -

1.57% over the previous year. During 2012-13 and 2013-14, GSDP grew at 5.34% (2nd Revised Estimates) and 5.63% (1st Revised Estimates) respectively. The State economy is expected to register growth of 0.40% (advanced estimates) at current prices during 2014-15 as compared to 13.85% in 2013-14 (1st Revised estimates) and 12.81% in 2012-13 (2nd Revised Estimates). At Constant (2004-05) Prices growth in GSDP of J&K State is expected to register a negative growth of -1.57% during the year 2014-15 as compared to 5.63% during 2013-14. The lesser growth rate during 2014-15 is mainly attributed to floods of September, 2014, which has shattered the economy of the state affecting particularly Kashmir valley *(JK Economic Survey, 2014-15)*.

The survey conducted by the State during 2007- 08 put the BPL population at 21.63 percent. The survey on employment – unemployment carried out by NSSO provides estimates on various characteristics pertaining to employment and unemployment at the National as well as State level. The latest NSS Survey- 68th round conducted during July, 2011 – June, 2012 throughout the country constitutes an important source of information on unemployment. Unemployment rate as per Usual Principal Status (UPS) in J&K has come down from 5.3% to 4.9% during the period July, 2009 to June, 2012 i.e. (66th & 68th Round of NSS respectively) which is still higher than the unemployment rate of 2.7% at all India level *(JK Economic Survey, 2014-15)*.

Profile of the District Kupwara

The Kupwara district is situated at an altitude of 5300 feet, above sea level. The district has varied topography with a hilly terrain, only the southern parts of the district are plain. The district is located at 34.3 degree to 35.5 degree latitude in the north and 73.4 to 74.9 degree longitude in the east. The geographical area of the district is 2,379 sq .kms and the density is 366 persons per sq.km. The district consists of three tehsils namely Kupwara, Handwara and Karnah.

Table 2: Kupwara: Adminstrative Profile

Administrative Unit	Kupwara	State(J&K)
Tehsils	3	82
C.D Blocks	11	142

Towns	2	86
Villages	367	6652
Panchayats	356	4128

Source: Directorate of economics & statistics, J&K.

In table 1.3, the administrative profile of the district and state is presented. The total number of tehsils in the state is 82 whereas the district Kupwara has 3 tehsils. Respectively, the numbers of villages are 367 in the district and 6652 in the state. Similarly, the C.D blocks in the state are 142 whereas there are 11C.D blocks in the district Kupwara.

Demographic profile of Kupwara

The data related to population was collected from secondary sources, which reveals that the district kupwara is predominantly a rural society with almost 88% rural population. This shows the significance of MGNREGS for sustaining the livelihood security of the people in the district. The literacy rate of kupwara is 64.51% which is below that of the state 67.16% *(Census, 2011)*. The literacy rate is very low among female folks of the district, only 50.95% women are literate.

The total population of the district as per census 2011 is 870354 persons. Table 3 reveals that the population consists of 474190 males and 396164 females. The rural sector of the district is inhabited by 412038 males and 353587 females spread over 353 inhabited villages where as the urban sector is inhabited by 104729 persons which consists of 412038 males and 353587 females. The rural population is 88% of the total population and urban population is just 12%. The sex ratio is 835 in the district which is lower that the state wide sex ratio of 889.

Table 3: Population of Kupwara:- Male-Female; Rural-Urban

		Population	870354
Population	Total	Males	474190
		Females	396164
	Urban (12%) State(27.38)	Population	104729
		Males	62152
		Females	42577

		Population	765625
	Rural (88%)	Males	412038
		Females	353587
Sex Ratio (females/1000)	State	889	
	Kupwara	835	

Source: Analysis of District Census Handbook India, 2011.

Socio-economic profile of the district Kupwara.

The population of social minorities such as scheduled castes and scheduled tribes in district kupwara is very low at 0.12% and 8.08% respectively *(census, 2011)*. Table 4 presents the population figures for SC's and ST's in the district. The absolute numbers of scheduled castes population is meager 1048 and scheduled tribe population is 70,352 in the district. The population for social minorities particularly SC's & ST's in Kashmir division is generally low.

Table 4: Population of SC & ST in Kupwara – Gender Wise

		Number	**Percentage**
Scheduled Caste Population (Kupwara)	Total	1,048	0.12
	Male	1,046	0.22
	Female	2	0.00
Scheduled Tribe population (Kupwara)	Total	70,352	8.08
	Male	36,913	7.78
	Female	33,439	8.44

Source: Analysis of DCHB India, 2011.

The sample district of kupwara is the second poorest district in Kashmir division with 32.55% of population falling below the poverty line *(J&K BPL Survey, 2008)*. The district has 40927 households below the poverty line. The economy of the district is broadly an agrarian one with very low presence of horticulture and other sectors. Therefore, the district is socially and economically very much backward (Socio-economic profile, DSEK, 2008).

The data in table 5 shows the number of working and non-working population of the state and district kupwara. The workers in J&K, both main and marginal workers, constitute 4,322,713 that are 34.47% of total population. The number of non-workers in the state is 8,218,589 with 65.53% of the total population. The total workers in kupwara are 229,064 constituting 26.32% of total population of the district. The percentage of non-workers in the district is huge 73.68% constituting 641,290. The data reveals huge dependency rate in J&K state and even higher dependency figures for the district.

Table 5: Workers and Non-workers of district Kupwara vis-à-vis J&K State

Workers and Non-Workers	Total Number (J&K)	Percentage	Total Number (Kupwara)	Percentage
Total Workers (Main and Marginal)	4,322,713	34.47	229,064	26.32
Main Workers	2,644,149	21.08	123,837	14.23
Marginal Workers	1,678,564	13.38	105,227	12.09
Non- Workers	8,218,589	65.53	641,290	73.68

Source: Analysis of District Census Handbook India, 2011.

The data in table 6 shows the occupational classification of workers in the state and district kupwara. The marginal and other workers constitute over 85% of total workforce in kupwara district. This reflects the backward character of the economy in the district. The employment in such occupations such as household sector and other marginal occupations generates merely a subsistence wage. Which is hardly enough for the family to take care of even the most basic necessities of life. The occupation classification of employment in the district and blocks provides a better context for understanding the outcomes of the scheme.

Table 6: Occupational Classification of Workers District Kupwara vis-à-vis J&K state

Category of Workers (Main & Marginal)	Total Number (J&K)	%age	Total Number (Kupwara)	%age
Cultivators	1,245,316	28.81	34,680	15.14
Agricultural Labourers	547,705	12.67	56,759	24.78
Workers in HH Industry	172,586	3.99	7,946	3.47
Other Workers	2,357,106	54.53	129,679	56.61

Source: Analysis of District Census Handbook India, 2011.   HH: Households

Profile of Sample Blocks in District Kupwara

The sample community development blocks of Trehgam and Langate are randomly selected from kupwara district. The socio-economic profile of the two blocks is presented below. The data in table 7 reveals the number of households in the sample blocks in Kupwara. The data shows that the block Langate is predominantly a rural sector with not even a single household in the semi-urban or urban area. In Trehgam block, out of the total 8988 households a great proportion of 7169 households fall in rural area, with only 1819 of households in urban sector of the block. The female population in block Trehgam is 47.09% of the total population and in Langate block 46.77% population is of women folks.

Table 7: Distribution of Male & Female Population of Sample Blocks

Block	Number HH		Total	Population		
	Rural	Urban		Female	Male	Total

Trehgam	7169	1819	8988	36655 (47.09%)	41169	77824
Langate	15641	0	15641	52660 (46.77%)	59916	112576

Source: Analysis of DCHB, Census India, 2011.

The distribution of literacy rates in Trehgam and Langate block presents stark inequality in-terms of male-female literacy divide across sample blocks. The total number of male literates in block Trehgam is 23,743 whereas the number of female literates is only 15,220. The number of female & male literates 59,299 is higher in block Langate than in block Trehgam that is 39,143.

Table 8: Literacy Rate Block-wise on Male-Female & Rural-Urban Basis

Blolck	Literate				Total Literate
	Rural		Urban		
	Male	Female	Male	Female	
Trehgam	16,095	10,538	7,648	4862	39,143
Langate	37,272	22,027	0	0	59,299

Source: Analysis of DCHB, Census India, 2011.

The data in table 9 shows the distribution of panchayats and villages in sample blocks of Trehgam and Langate in kupwara district. In block Trehgam, the total number of villages are 21 and Panchayats are 34 whereas, the number of panchayats in Langate block is 55 and 98 villages with one uninhabited village as per the census data of 2011.

Table 9: Block-wise Number of Halqa Panchayats and Villages

Block	Number of Panchayats	Number of Census Villages		
		Total	Inhabited	Uninhabited
Trehgam	34	21	21	0
Langate	55	98	97	1

Source: Analysis of DCHB, Census India, 2011.

Profile of District Poonch

The district of Poonch is situated at a distance of 246 kilometers North West of Jammu with an altitude of about 3287 ft. The district is surrounded by the Line of Control (LoC) from three sides and is separated from the Kashmir Valley by the mighty Peer Panchal Range in the North. Poonch has four Tehsils, namely, Mendhar, Surankote, Poonch and Mandi. These tahsils are further divided into 6 Community Development Blocks viz Poonch, Mandi, Mendhar, Balakote, Surankote and Buffliaz. The rural sector of the district is constituted of 178 villages out of which 8 are un-inhabited *(Census, 2011)*. The district of Poonch has an area of 1674.00 Sq Km. Its density i.e population per Sq. Km works out of 285. As per figures of 2011 Census, Poonch has returned a population of 476,835, constituting 3.8 % of the total population of the State Poonch ranks 11th in terms of population. The number of males and females is 251,899 and 224,936 respectively. Sex ratio i.e number of females per 1000 males works out to 893 which is slightly higher as compared to the corresponding ratio of the State 889.

Table 10: Administrative Profile of District Poonch

Administrative Unit	Number
Tehsils	4
Community Development Blocks	6
Towns	2
Villages	178 (8 uninhabited)
Panchayats	189

Source: Analysis of District Census Handbook, Poonch, 2011.

Figure 2: Map showing district Poonch

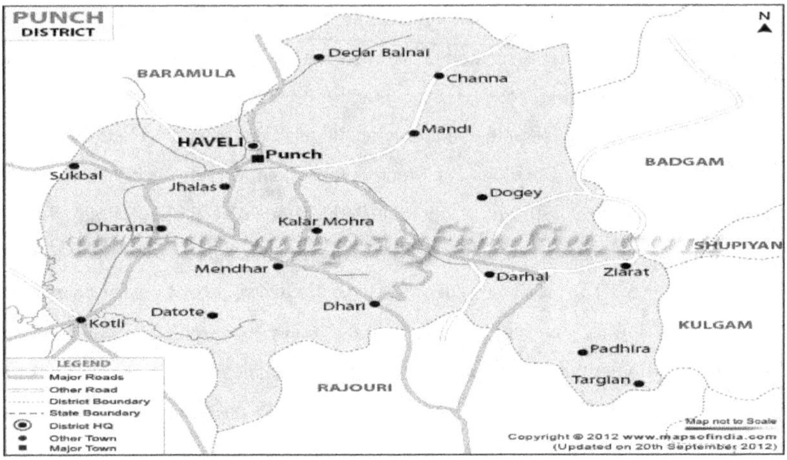

Source: www.mapsofindia.com

Demographic Profile of District Poonch

The data for population and its distribution across various dimensions such as male, female, rural- urban and sex ratio was collected from secondary sources. The total population of the district is 476,835 and male population is 251,899 where as female population is 224,936. The urban population is only 8.10% compared to 27.38% of the state. Therefore, about 92% of the population is living in rural sector which shows that Poonch district is predominantly a rural stronghold and the role of guaranteed wages schemes such as MGNREGS is pivotal for sustaining the livelihood security of these people. The sex ratio of 893, which is number of females per 1000 males, is above the state average of 889.

Table 11: Demographic profile of district Poonch

Population	Total	Population	476,835
		Males	251,899
		Females	224,936
	Urban (8.10%) State (27.38)	Population	38,630
		Males	22,125
		Females	16,505
	Rural (91.9%)	Population	438,205
		Males	229,774
		Females	208,431
Sex Ratio (females/1000)	State	889	
	Poonch	893	

Source: Analysis of District Census Handbook, Poonch, 2011.

Socio-economic Profile of District Poonch

The data in table 12 shows literacy rate 66.74% in district Poonch is slightly below than that of the state average of 68.74%. The male literacy rate in the district is 78.84% and female literacy rate is 53.19%, which is below than that of the female literacy rate in the state of J&K 58.01% female literates.

The population of socially backward communities such as scheduled castes and scheduled tribes is about 37.05%, which is relatively higher than the state average of about 20%.

Table 12: Literacy rates and SC, ST Population Gender Wise in District Poonch

			Number	Percentage
Literates		Total	261,724	66.74
		Male	163,333	78.84
		Female	98,391	53.19
Scheduled Caste Population		Total	556	0.12
		Male	406	0.16

	Female	150	0.07
	Total	176,101	36.93
Scheduled Tribe Population	Male	90,274	35.84
	Female	85,827	38.16

Source: *Analysis of District Census Handbook, Poonch, 2011.*

The sample district Poonch is the fourth poorest district in Jammu division with 33.67% of population below poverty line with estimated 0.242 lakh BPL household *(JK BPL Survey, 208-09)*. Besides, Poonch has an average population per branch of 14000 people making it the most backward district by this indicator followed by Kupwara & Budgam *(JK Economic Survey, 2014-15)*.

The data in table 13, shows that the total labour participation in district Poonch is 161,393 that is 33.85% of total population who can work. The non-working population is 66.15% of the total labour force which is slightly higher than the state average of non-working population of 65.53% in 2011. This again reflects the dismal rate of labour participation, and the need to provide gainful work to people who are willing to work in unskilled or semi-skilled jobs. Therefore, given the low labour participation rates in the state of J&K in general and the higher low labour participation in sample districts of kupwara and poonch in particular, the need for the 100 days work guarantee scheme such as MGNREGS is greater in these districts for providing livelihood and sustaining that livelihood security for the poor people.

Table 13: Workers and Non-Workers Population in District Poonch Vis-à-vis J&K

Workers and Non-Workers	Total Number (J&K)	Percentage	Total Number (Poonch)	Percentage
Total Workers (Main and Marginal)	4,322,713	34.47	161,393	33.85
Main Workers	2,644,149	21.08	73,247	15.36

| Marginal Workers | 1,678,564 | 13.38 | 88,146 | 18.49 |
| Non- Workers | 8,218,589 | 65.53 | 315,442 | 66.15 |

Source: Analysis of District Census Handbook, Poonch, 2011.

The occupational distribution of working population in Poonch is shown in table 14. The data shows that 33.62% of the working population is employed in cultivation sector, 19.57% as agricultural labourers and 2.44% in household industry respectively. The significant point is that around 55% of working population in Poonch is employed in primary sector of the economy which is more than that of the state average of around 45%.

Table 14: Occupational Distribution of Workers in District Poonch Vis-à-vis J&K

Category of Workers (Main & Marginal)	Total Number (J&K)	Percentage	Total Number (Poonch)	Percentage
Cultivators	1,245,316	28.81	54,264	33.62
Agricultural Labourers	547,705	12.67	31,583	19.57
Workers in Household industry	172,586	3.99	3,930	2.44
Other Workers	2,357,106	54.53	71,616	44.37

Source: Analysis of District Census Handbook, Poonch, 2011.

Profile of Sample Blocks in District Poonch

The total population of the block Poonch is 83,600 with 47.60% female population. The total of 16,375 households in Poonch block is in the rural sector. The population of Surankot, block in Poonch district of Jammu division, is 90,298 with 47.48% female population and all its households are residing in villages. This data in table 15 and coupled with 1.92 lakh households under below poverty line (BPL) in Jammu region *(JK BPL Survey, 2008-09)* yet again highlights the significance of the MGNREGS, a 100 days job guarantee scheme for this rural community.

Table 15: Distribution of Population and Households in Sample Blocks, Region & Gender Wise

Block	Number of Households		Total	Population		
	Rural	Urban		Female	Male	Total
Poonch	16,375	0	16,375	39,796 (47.60%)	43,804	83,600
Surankot	17,045	0	17,045	42,881 (47.48%)	47,417	90,298

Source: Analysis of District Census Handbook, Block Poonch & Surankot, 2011.

The data in table 16 shows the distribution of literates among male and female, rural and urban population in sample blocks of Poonch and Surankot. The total literate population in block Poonch is 47,004 which is 56.22% of total population whereas in block Surankot the total literate population is 44,965 with female literate population of 16,525. Therefore, it is quite evident that a sizable population in both blocks of Poonch & Surankot is illiterate.

Table 16: Distribution of Literacy Rates in Block Poonch and Surankote

Blolck	Literates				Total Literates
	Rural		Urban		
	Male	Female	Male	Female	
Poonch	28,640	18,740	0	0	47,004
Surankote	28,440	16,525	0	0	44,965

Source: Analysis of District Census Handbook, Poonch, 2011.

The data in table 17 reveals that the scheduled tribe (ST) population in both the blocks is sizable. In block Poonch, the total population of scheduled tribe community is 39,973 whereas in Surankot ST Population is 45,537. The population of scheduled caste communities in both these blocks is insignificant. It is quite evident that the role of MGNREGS is significant in providing livelihood security to these socially backward communities in these blocks.

Table 17: Distribution of SC & ST Population Region Wise in Block Poonch & Surankote

Block	SC			ST		
	Male	Female	Total	Male	Female	Total
Poonch	58	15	73	20,566	19,407	39,973
Surankote	9	0	9	23,523	22,014	45,537

Source: Analysis of District Census Handbook, Block Poonch & Surankote, 2011.

Performance of MGNREGS at J&K State Level

The MGNREGS scheme has been launched in J&K from February, 2006 initially in three districts namely Doda, Poonch and Kupwara (Phase-I). The scheme has been subsequently extended to two more districts viz., Jammu and Anantnag from April, 2007 (Phase-II). However, at present, the MGNREGS scheme is under implementation in all the districts of the State w.e.f 01.04.2008.

The main objective of this scheme is to provide 100 days of guaranteed unskilled wage employment to each rural household opting for it *(MGNREGA, 2005-06)*. The scheme is demand driven, self targeting and envisages coverage of not only BPL families but also above poverty line (APL) families. The households who volunteer to do manual work are issued job cards and are paid for their work in accordance with minimum wages notified by the state under The J&K Minimum Wages Act, 1948. The minimum wages fixed for these categories of workers vide SRO No. 304 dated 01-10- 2009, is Rs 225 for skilled, Rs 175 for semi-skilled workers and Rs 150 for unskilled workers per day.

The performance of the scheme has been dismal which explicitly clear from the data extracted from secondary sources. The data in table 18 shows the total number of job cards issued as on 12 December 2016 is 12.95 lakhs and less than 10 lakh active job cards. The problem with the implementation of MGNREGS scheme in J&K is that the active job card holders is less than the total number of active workers. This shows people lack awareness about the right to hold a job card once they apply for work. The SC and ST's are about 19.50% of total active workers in MGNREGS labour force in J&K.

Table 18: Distribution of MGNREGS Job Cards in J&K

Job Cards	
Total No. of Job Cards issued[In Lakhs]	12.95
Total No. of Workers [In Lakhs]	23.02
Total No. of Active Job Cards[In Lakhs]	9.38
Total No. of Active Workers[In Lakhs]	14.12
SC worker against active workers[%]	5.38
ST worker against active workers[%]	14.14

Source: *www.nrega.nic.in*, *accessed on 12/12/2016.*

Table 19 & Figure 2 shows that the average person days generated has continuously declined from 56.54 days in 2012-13 to 48.45 average Man-days in 2015-16. The data points for average man days generated is substantially lower than the MGNREGS mandated guaranteed 100 days of employment to every household in rural India. The problem is further compounded by the fact that only 34,675 households completed 100 days of employment in 2015-16 against 6.53 lakh households worked for the same period. However, the performance on employment to socially backward communities such as SC & ST and women has been modest to good, considering the combined person days generated is above 47% of total person days generated in 2015-16. The MGNREGS provides 33% reservation for women in various works executed under the scheme. But, the problem is that the women person days have not gone beyond 27% of the total person days generated throughout the history of MGNREGS in J&K state.

Table 19: Performance of MGNREGS By Person days Generated in J&K

Person Days Generated	FY 2016-17	FY 2015-16	FY 2014-15	FY 2013-14	FY 2012-13
Persondays Generated so far [In Lakhs]	86.42	316.39	121.09	337.83	365.56
SC persondays % as of total persondays	6.49	5.83	4.69	5.99	5.8
ST persondays % as of total persondays	20.09	16.81	20.13	15.91	15.37
Women Persondays out of Total (%)	26.14	25.28	25.28	23.14	19.88
Average days of Employment provided per Household	35.2	48.45	36.44	51.4	56.54
Total No of HHs completed 100 Days of Wage Employment	3,037	34,675	7,858	66,639	69,381
Total Households Worked [In Lakhs]	2.46	6.53	3.32	6.57	6.47
Total Individuals Worked [In Lakhs]	3.21	9.44	4.31	9.16	9.57
Differently abled persons worked	1078	6007	1832	6655	6469

Source: www.nrega.nic.in, accessed on 12/12/2016.

Figure 3: Average Employment Days Generated Over a Period of Time

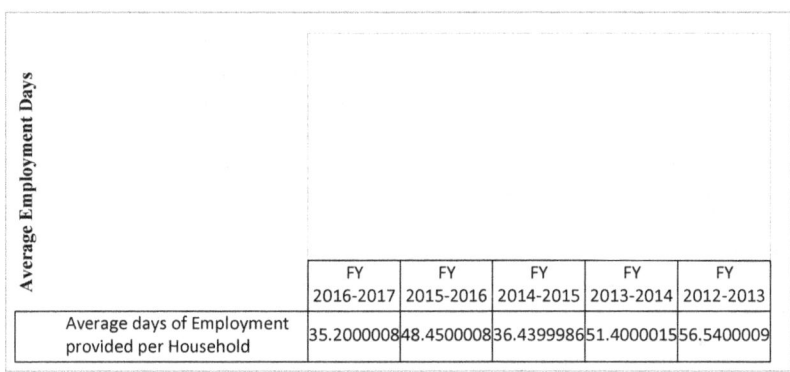

	FY 2016-2017	FY 2015-2016	FY 2014-2015	FY 2013-2014	FY 2012-2013
Average days of Employment provided per Household	35.2000008	48.4500008	36.4399986	51.4000015	56.5400009

The planning and execution of MGNREGS in J&K has been poor considering the percentage of works completed to works taken up for execution. The data in table 20 shows physical performance of the scheme in J&K, the number of works completed in 2015-16 is only 84,226 against 1.88 lakh works taken up for execution in the state. This reveals monumental mismatch and poor execution and implementation of the scheme in the state. The number of ongoing works has been continuously rising from 0.9 lakh in 2012-13 to 1.04 lakh in 2015-16.

Table 20: Physical Performance of MGNREGS in J&K

Works (In lakhs)	2016-17	2015-16	2014-15	2013-14	2012-13
Total No. of Works Takenup	1.25	1.88	1.59	1.76	1.48
Number of Ongoing Works	1	1.04	1.28	1.21	0.9
Number of Completed Works	24,969	84,226	31,652	54,792	57,691
% of Expenditure on Agriculture & Agriculture Allied Works	44.19	45.1	45.61	42.56	41.68

Source: www.nrega.nic.in, accessed on 12/12/2016.

The financial performance of MGNREGS in J&K state is presented in table 21 & fig. 4. The total funds available for MGNREGS in the state in 2015-16 is Rs 79033.13 Lakh, out of this 97.24% has been spent on various works and wages to workers. This shows the efficiency in utilization of available funds for the scheme. However, the problem of non-disbursal of wages to workers on time has been increasing as can be seen in figure 1.6. The wage liability was highest for financial year 2016-17 of Rs 12643 Lakhs till 12/12/2016. The total wage liability for 2015-16 is Rs 9,936.45 Lakh which is a staggering figure and a sign of inefficiency of the implementation machinery. The poor participation by rural households as reflected in low average man-days generated is largely due to non-disbursal of wages on time. The wage liability bill has been continuously going up from Rs 143.65 lakhs in FY 2012-13 to Rs 9,936.45 in FY 2015-16 and upward trend in wage liability can be seen in figure 1.6.

Table 21: Financial Performance for MGNREGS in J&K

Financial Progress	2016-17	2015-16	2014-15	2013-14	2012-13
Total center Release (Lakhs)	73611.03	54504.61	40456.98	67253.87	69338.02
Total Availability (Lakhs)	78897.17	79033.13	46815.79	73141.45	70054.91
Percentage Utilization	56.68	97.24	84.1	104.51	121.81
TotalExp(Lakhs.)	44,718.41	76,853.05	39,372.93	76,438.06	85,334
Wages(Rs. Lakhs)	24,645.28	34,126.72	17,865.7	39,584.84	43,138.95
Material and skilled Wages(Rs. Lakhs)	17,705.48	37,331.82	18,028.75	33,314.19	39,463.57
Material (%)	41.81	52.24	50.23	45.7	47.78
Total Adm Expenditure (lakhs.)	2,367.65	5,394.52	3,478.48	3,539.03	2,731.48
Admin Exp (%)	5.29	7.02	8.83	4.63	3.2
Wage Liability(Lakhs.)	12,643.94	9,936.45	2,392.03	1,784.74	143.65

Average Cost Per Day Per Person (In Rs.)	284.41	302.29	280.91	232.8	244.74

Source: www.nrega.nic.in, accessed on 12/12/2016.

Figure 4: Trend for Wage Liability in MGNREGS

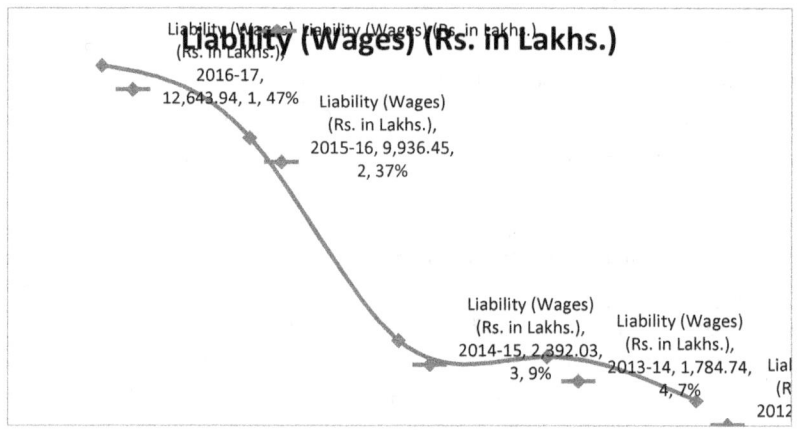

Performance of MGNREGS in Sample District Kupwara

The total number of job cards issued till December 2016 is 0.85 lakh and the number of active job cards is only 0.67 lakh. Which reflects the poor implementation of the scheme as the workers should be issued job cards once they demand work which isn't the case as is reflected by the total workers worked. The data in table 3.3 also shows that the total number of active workers is only 1.16 lakh which is poor considering a majority of the population puts up in villages. The small proportion of SC and ST workers is due to the small population of these social groups in the district.

Table 22: Performance of MGNREGS in District Kupwara By Job Cards

Job Cards	
Total No. of Job Cards issued[In Lakhs]	0.85
Total No. of Workers[In Lakhs]	1.57

Total No. of Active Job Cards[In Lakhs]	0.67
Total No. of Active Workers[In Lakhs]	1.16
SC worker against active workers[%]	0.1
ST worker against active workers[%]	2.66

Source: www.nrega.nic.in, accessed on 12/12/2016.

The person days generated is a good indicator of the performance of the scheme. The data in table 23 shows that the total person days generated for 2012-13 is 20.32 lakh which is down to 6.97 lakh in 2014-15. The interesting data point in table 3.4 is the percentage of women person days to total person days is 29.37% person days, which is good considering the cultural factors of the region. The figure 1.7 depicts that the average person days generated for 2012-13 is 55.38 which has gone down to 48.53 in 2015-16 which is way below than the MGNREGA Act 2005-06 mandated guaranteed 100 days of unskilled employment to rural households in a year. The poor implementation of the scheme is also reflected by the small value of total No of HHs completed 100 Days of wage employment. The data for this variable is only 2,388 households in 2015-16 against 0.44 lakh households worked for the same period.

Table 23: Performance of MGNREGS By Person Days Generated in District Kupwara

Person Days Generated	FY 2016-17	FY 2015-16	FY 2014-15	FY 2013-14	FY 2012-13
Persondays Generated so far [In Lakhs]	2.49	21.12	6.97	26.94	20.32
SC Persondays % as of total Persondays	0.31	0.14	0.1	0.11	0.03
ST Persondays % as of total Persondays	3.66	2.78	2.92	3.04	0.98
Women Persondays out of Total (%)	29.37	27.03	26.42	24.27	15.23
Average days of employment provided per	29.7	48.53	35.83	55	55.38

Household					
Total No of HHs completed 100 Days of Wage Employment	70	2,388	461	4,605	2,829
Total Households Worked [In Lakhs]	0.08	0.44	0.19	0.49	0.37
Total Individuals Worked [In Lakhs]	0.14	0.75	0.31	0.8	0.52
Differently abled persons worked	20	57	14	73	27

Source: *www.nrega.nic.in*, accessed on 12/12/2016.

Figure 5: Average Days of Employment in Kupwara Under MGNREGS

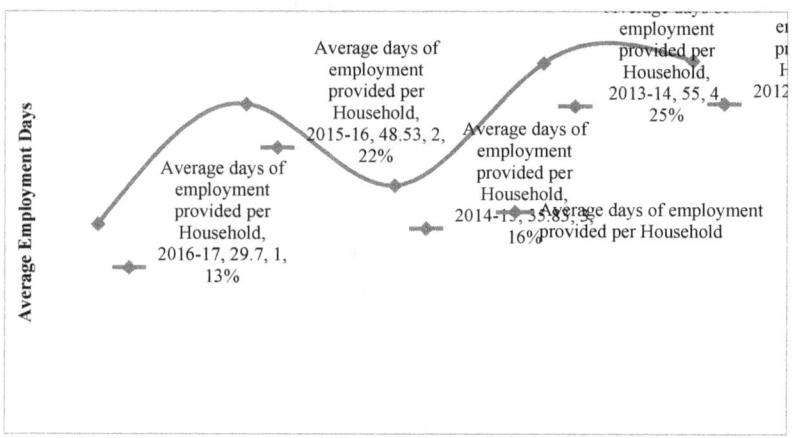

The data in table 3.5 shows the physical performance of the scheme in district kupwara. The total number of works taken up for 2015-16 is 0.17 lakh whereas the total number of completed works for the same period is only 10,144 which is glaring evidence of the dismal implementation of the scheme in the district. The data for the previous years for the disparity in works taken up and works completed is worse than for 2015-16. The poor implementation and execution of works is primarily on account of the lackadaisical approach of the officials coupled with geographic, climatic and political factors which accentuates the problem. As is evident by the 6-7 months productive period and for rest of the year the climatic conditions are just impossible for any meaningful execution of works.

Table 24: Physical Performance of MGNREGS in District Kupwara

Works	FY 2016-17	FY 2015-16	FY 2014-15	FY 2013-14	FY 2012-13
Total No. of Works Taken up (New+Spill Over)[In Lakhs]	0.08	0.17	0.13	0.16	0.1
Number of Ongoing Works [In Lakhs]	0.06	0.07	0.11	0.12	0.07
Number of Completed Works	2,447	10,144	1,561	3,900	3,397
% of Expenditure on Agriculture & Agriculture Allied Works	53.16	57.06	47.4	47.71	41.55

Source: www.nrega.nic.in, accessed on 12/12/2016.

The data for financial performance of the scheme in kupwara district is depicted in table 3.6. The total expenditure for the year 2012-13 is Rs 6,263.48 lakhs which has gone down to Rs 2,392.57 lakhs in year 2014-15. The wages bill has also been declining from Rs 2,577.39 lakhs in FY 2012-13 to Rs 2,129.27 lakhs in FY 2015-16. The problem is that the wages are not disbursed to workers on time as reflected by the data on wages liability. The unpaid wages for the FY 2015-16 is Rs 368.79 lakhs which is poor and it partially explains the dismal implementation of the scheme in the district given the poor participation of rural households and the problem is compounded by the low wages of around Rs 130-155 per day compared to market wages rates in excess of Rs 200 per day. Again, the data on wages disbursed to workers within 15 days is dismal 4.67% for 2015-16. In nutshell, the financial performance of the scheme in district Kupwara is abject and needs drastic improvement for desired outcomes from the scheme.

Table 25: Financial Performance For MGNREGS in Kupwara

Financial Performance	FY 2016-17	FY 2015-16	FY 2014-15	FY 2013-14	FY 2012-13
Total Exp (Rs. in Lakhs.)	2,924.58	5,437.34	2,392.57	5,354.73	6,263.48
Wages (Rs. In Lakhs)	1,774.85	2,129.27	1,463.20	2,879.62	2,577.39
Material and skilled Wages (Rs. In Lakhs)	974.31	2,954.90	730.61	2,258.28	3,610.69
Material(%)	35.44	58.12	33.3	43.95	58.35
Total Adm Expenditure (Rs. in Lakhs.)	175.42	53.17	198.76	216.84	75.41
% Payments generated within 15 days	17.83	4.67	2.74	13.83	26.37
Liability (Wages) (Rs. in Lakhs.)	308.48	368.79	143.91	113.71	7.38

Source: *www.nrega.nic.in*, accessed on 12/12/2016.

Performance of MGNREGS in Sample Blocks of District Kupwara

The performance of MGNREGS in block Langate of district kupwara is shown in table 3.7. The person days generated for FY 2012-13 is 2,58,268 which has drastically gone down to 38,837 for FY 2015-16 and worse for FY 2014-15. The percentage of women person days generated to total person days is only 9.68% for FY 2015-16.

Average person days per household in the block is only 24.44 in FY 2014-15 and gone up to 44.28 person days per household in 2015-16 which is still far off the 100 days guaranteed wage employment to rural households. The data for the employment is worse as we look at the number of households which have completed 100 days of wage employment is only 47 against 877 households worked for FY 2015-16.

Table 26: Distribution Of Person Days Generated in Langate Block

Person Days Generated	FY 2016-17	FY 2015-16	FY 2014-15	FY 2013-14	FY 2012-13
Total Person Days Generated So Far	4,977	38,837	3,739	3,06,786	2,58,268
SC Person Days % of Total PDG	0	0	0	0	0.1
ST Person Days % of Total PDG	0	0	0	0.04	0.04
Women Person Days % of Total PDG	7.84	9.68	7.44	8.75	4.27
Average Man Days Per HH	23.7	44.28	24.44	51.82	56.12
Total No of HHs completed 100 Days of Wage Employment	3	47	0	471	284
Total Households Worked	210	877	153	5,920	4,602
Total Individuals Worked	267	1,173	181	7,757	5,481
Differently abled persons worked	1	1	0	3	1

Source: www.nrega.nic.in, accessed on 12/12/2016.

The physical performance of the scheme in sample block Langate is reflected in table 3.8. The total number of works taken up for FY 2012-13 is 1,059 against only 439 completed works. This yet again reflects the poor execution and implementation of the scheme in district kupwara in general and sample block Langate in particular. The data for the work completion is poor for all the years under analysis. The poor implementation of the scheme is a result of a combination of factors as observed from the primary survey in sample districts and blocks. The fundamental factor being the official inefficiency in planning and execution of works coupled with the lack of decentralization of power to panchayats in the state and poor staffing for the scheme as most of lower level staff at execution level such as Programme officers (PO's) and Village level workers

(VLW's) work on tenure basis and hence lack the autonomy and power needed for efficient planning and execution. The corruption and political interference also result into poor implementation of the scheme.

Table 27: Physical Performance Of MGNREGS in Sample Block Langate

Works	FY 2016-17	FY 2015-16	FY 2014-15	FY 2013-14	FY 2012-13
Total No. of Works Takenup (New+Spill Over)	171	210	144	1,588	1,059
Number of Ongoing Works	54	156	144	1,257	620
Number of Completed Works	117	54	0	331	439
% of Expenditure on Agriculture & Agriculture Allied Works	25.9	34.91	28.13	32.26	36.4

Source: www.nrega.nic.in, accessed on 13/12/2016.

The performance in terms of person days generated in block Trehgam has drastically declined from 1, 71,530 in FY 2012-13 to only 60,121 in FY 2015-16 which is about 50% dip in employment generation in the scheme. The percentage of women person days as proportion of total person days generated has seen a considerable growth from 5.8% in FY 2012-13 to 37.82% in FY 2015-16.

The wage employment provided to rural households in Trehgam is far off from the MGNREGS mandated 100 days in a year. The data in table 3.9 shows that the average days of wage employment provided per household is just 54.51 in FY 2015-16.

The execution of scheme is dismal across the state of J&K and sample block Trehgam is no exception to that. Interms of physical performance of MGNREGS the gap between the works taken up for execution and works completed is widening. In FY 2013-14, a total of 1669 works were taken up for execution out of which only 5 works were completed and in FY 2015-16, 753 works were taken up for execution only 550 were completed. Therefore, there is an ample evidence to suggest that the scheme is poorly implemented in the block and the same holds true for other sample districts and blocks as has been analyzed in previous sections.

Table 28: Performance of MGNREGS in Block Trehgam of District Kupwara

Performance	FY 2016-17	FY 2015-16	FY 2014-15	FY 2013-14	FY 2012-13
Person-days Generated(PDG)					
Total PDG	785	60,121	20,412	3,38,556	1,71,530
SC PDG % of Total PDG	0	0	0	0	0
ST PDG % of Total PDG	0	0	0	1.13	0.87
Women PDG Out of Total (%)	39.24	37.82	37.74	25.37	5.8
Avg. Days of Employment Per HH	31.4	54.51	41.24	63.06	68.31
Physical Performance					
Total No. of Works Takenup (New+Spill Over)	204	753	651	1,669	606
Number of Completed Works	4	550	75	5	18
% of Expenditure on Agriculture & Agriculture Allied Works	60.97	68.05	54.87	52.91	46.6
Financial Performance					
Total Exp (Rs. in Lakhs.)	83.15	232.01	85.52	665	690.16
Wages (Rs. In Lakhs)	30.89	98.3	32.32	368.52	288
Liability(Wages) (Lakhs.	1.29	6.59	4.75	30.68	0.02
% Payments within 15 days	0	1.35	0	16.23	4.01

Source: *www.nrega.nic.in*, accessed on 16/12/2016.   HH: Household

The data in table 29 depicts the performance of the scheme in district Poonch, the total person days generated in FY 2015-16 is 21.9 lakhs which is lower than 28.06 lakhs in FY 2012-13. The total number of households who have worked for 100 days is only 3400 out of total thirty nine thousand (39000) households who have worked for the same period under MGNREGS in Poonch. The performance on other parameters such as works taken up and works completed ratio and wages paid within 15 days and wages unpaid liability figures is purely dismal and unproductive.

In FY 2015-16, a total of twenty thousand (20,000) works were taken up for execution and just over eight thousand (8000) works were completed. The inefficiency of wage payments is reflected by a mere 3.99% wages payments within 15 days of work in FY 2015-16. The decreasing allocation of funds coupled with low & delayed wages and poor planning of the is responsible for the dismal performance of the scheme in district poonch.

Table 29: Performance of MGNREGS in District Poonch

Performance	FY 2016-17	FY 2015-16	FY 2014-15	FY 2013-14	FY 2012-13
Person-days Generated(PDG)					
Total PDG (Lakhs)	5.36	21.9	11.21	21.3	28.06
SC PDG % of Total PDG	0.09	0.12	0.12	0.07	0.03
ST PDG % of Total PDG	30.77	33.83	34.7	33.25	34.09
Women PDG of Total (%)	28.4	27.7	27.27	22.017	15.13
Avg. Days of Employment Per HH	39.04	55.83	39.63	53.18	67.7
Total No of HH Completed 100 Days	368	3,400	1,081	3,246	7,575
Total Households Worked [In Lakhs]	0.14	0.39	0.28	0.4	0.41

Physical Performance					
Total No. of Works Takenup	0.14	0.2	0.16	0.13	0.15
Number of Completed Works	2,536	8,023	774	1,438	9,899
% Exp. on Agriculture & Agriculture Allied Works	50.04	51.6	65.81	72.64	54.26
Financial Performance					
Total Exp (Rs. in Lakhs.)	3,201.95	3,668.46	2,717.59	4,857.53	4,726.6
Wages (Rs. In Lakhs)	2,063.56	1,953.94	1,521.96	2,874.29	2,450.31
Liability (Wages) Lakhs	759.57	1,044.73	360.62	101.59	8.69
% Payments within 15 days	5.95	3.99	12.18	19.46	65.48

Source: www.nrega.nic.in, accessed on 17/12/2016.   HH: Household

The performance of MGNREGS in block Poonch of sample distric poonch is depicted in table 30. The total Person-days generated (PDG) in FY 2012-13 was 4, 86,977 which has declined to 1,62,260 PDG in FY 2015-16. The women's share in total PDG in FY 2015-16 was 34.07% which is up from 18.6% in FY 2012-13. Therefore, the performance of the block on women's work participation parameter is fairly to the satisfaction of the Act guidelines.

The physical performance of the scheme is reflected in total works completed in FY 201-16 is 1,133 out of total 1,677 works taken up for execution for the same period. The budget allocation of funds on agriculture and allied activities has gone down from over 72% in FY 2012-13 to 53.94% in FY 2015-16 which partially explains the poor works completion in sample districts and blocks.

Table 31: Performance of MGNREGS in Block Poonch of District Poonch

Performance	FY 2016-17	FY 2015-16	FY 2014-15	FY 2013-14	FY 2012-13
Person-days Generated(PDG)					
Total PDG	16,078	1,62,260	93,606	3,91,520	4,86,977

SC PDG % of Total PDG	0	0.02	0.07	0.02	0.07
ST PDG % of Total PDG	49.12	45.22	42.95	44.56	46.74
Women PDG Out of Total (%)	31.11	34.07	35.61	29.36	18.6
Avg. Days of Employment Per HH	28.16	48.76	29.39	53	65.28
Physical Performance					
Total No. of Works Takenup	689	1,677	1,314	1,921	2,566
Number of Completed Works	102	1,133	59	443	2,540
Financial Performance					
Total Exp. (Lakhs.)	247.11	385.43	359.91	980.72	817.45
Wages (Rs. In Lakhs)	156.43	133.66	184.97	617.22	392.3
Liability(Wages) (lakhs)	18.77	53.61	2.19	0.74	0.26
% Payments Generated within 15 days	8.74	3.36	29.02	7.12	60.48

Source: www.nrega.nic.in, accessed on 17/12/2016.   HH: Household

The total Person days generated in sample block Surankote in FY 2012-13 is 4, 86,424 which has declined to 2,24,217 in FY 2015-16. The percentage of women in work participation has steadily declined from 28.22% to 23.76% in FY 2015-16. The average days of wage employment provided to rural households in Surankote is 55.47 days which is up from 36.2 average days in FY 2014-15. The proportion of wage employment to social minorities such as ST's is modest given the population of ST's in block Surankote is around 50% in 2011-12.

The ratio between works taken up and works completed is considerable as can be seen from the table 4.2. The works taken up for execution in FY 2015-16 is 2,366 out of which only 1,286 have been completed. The possible reasons for this growing work incompletion rate are many such as declining allocation of funds to labour intensive works in agriculture and allied activities as evident from the relevant data in the table 4.2. The allocation of funds to agriculture and allied activities has gone down from 59.97 in FY 2014-15 to 16.2% in FY 2016-17. The inefficiency and poor implementation of the scheme is also reflected in lower participation of women in work, delay in wage payment and growing liabilities on wage side due to non disbursal of wages on time and low wages compared to prevailing market wage rates.

Table 32: Performance of MGNREGS in Block Surankote of District Poonch

Performance	2016-17	2015-16	2014-15	2013-14	2012-13
Person-days Generated(PDG)					
Total PDG	28,592	2,24,217	1,15,576	3,56,762	4,86,424
SC PDG % of Total PDG	0	0.01	0.01	0	0
ST PDG % of Total PDG	34.12	36.29	34.35	35.56	43.81
Women PDG Out of Total (%)	23.09	23.76	28.22	19.14	11.91
Avg. Days of Employment Per HH	37.47	55.47	36.2	48.04	65.38
Physical Performance					
Total No. of Works Takenup	1,305	2,366	2,100	3,183	3,399
Number of Completed Works	259	1,286	102	101	1,390
% of Expenditure on Agriculture & Agriculture Allied Works	29.75	16.2	59.97	58.34	38.06
Financial Performance					
Total Exp (Rs. in Lakhs.)	236.19	357.05	255.9	828.33	932.79
Wages (Rs. In Lakhs)	167.44	195.14	126.66	467.44	410.43
Liability (Wages) (Rs. in Lakhs.	48.49	150.66	59.72	21.73	0

Source: www.nrega.nic.in, accessed on 17/12/2016.   HH: Household

Figure 5: Average Employment Days in Block Surankote

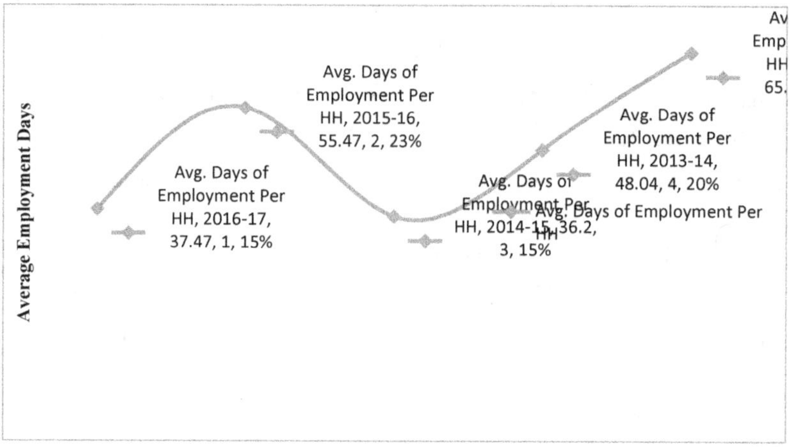

[Chart showing average employment days per household:
- Avg. Days of Employment Per HH, 2016-17, 37.47, 1, 15%
- Avg. Days of Employment Per HH, 2015-16, 55.47, 2, 23%
- Avg. Days of Employment Per HH, 2014-15, 36.2, 3, 15%
- Avg. Days of Employment Per HH, 2013-14, 48.04, 4, 20%
- Avg. Days of Employment Per HH, 65.]

3.5 Implementation Mechanism of MGNREGS

MGNREGS is the largest wage employment guarantee programme in the world with the primary aim of providing 100 days wage employment guarantee to rural households in India. The other objectives include creation of sustainable assets, protecting the environment, financial inclusion and empowering women by providing 33% reservation in wage employment (MGNEREGA, 2005-06). These objectives cannot be achieved without the effective and efficient implementation involving all the stakeholders. The implementation mechanism of MGNREGS is presented in Figure 1.9.

Tier V: Central Government: The Ministry of Rural Development, Government of India is the nodal agency for MGNREGS implementation. The Central Government has set up Central Employment Guarantee Council for MGNREGA implementation besides independent evaluation & monitoring of the scheme.

Tier IV: State Government: The state government is an important cog in the implementation mechanism of MGNREGS. It is responsible for setting up the State Employment Guarantee Council which acts as an advisor to the Government on implementation, monitoring & evaluation of the programme in the state.

Tier III: District Panchayat: The Act envisions an important role for panchayats at all levels such as district block and village. The district panchayat is tasked with role of coordinating the implemenatation of scheme at district level by preparing the district annual plan & the five year perspective plans in consultation with Gram & Block Panchayats.

Tier II: Block Panchayat: The Panchayat at the block level deals with the implementation of the programme by supervising and coordinating the work with village panchayats. It also looks after updating the data under the MGNREGS works, muster, job cards etc.

Tier I: Gram Panchayat: This is the Tier I agency in the sense that it is responsible for registration of households , issuance of job cards, muster roll preparation & maintenance, providing work, social audit and and selection of and implementation of most of the works.

Fig. 6: Implementation structure of MGNREGA

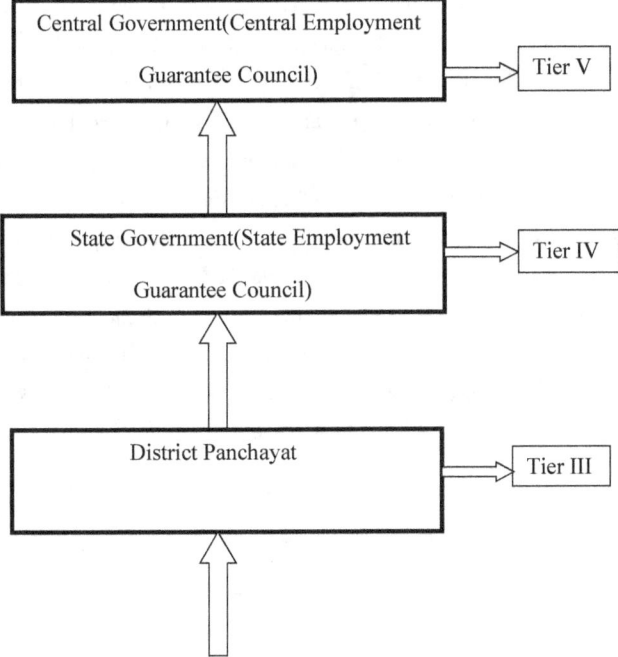

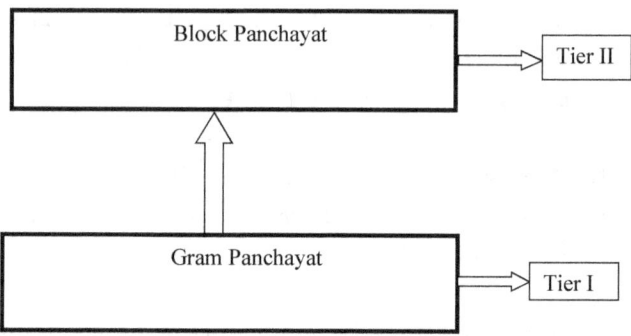

Implementation Mechanism of MGNREGS in J&K State

The implementation agencies in the state are central employment guarantee council, state employment guarantee council which has been set up under section 12 of the central act which is known as J&K State Employment Guarantee Council (JKSEGC) for the purposes of monitoring & reviewing the implementation of this act at the state level. The MGNREGS Act envisages an important role for the Panchayats at the district, block and village level. In case of J&K State since Intermediate/Block & District level Panchayats are not in place, therefore the district annual plan under MGNREGA is put up before District Development Board for approval. As per guidelines, by 31st December each year district body should approve the annual MGNREGA plan for next financial year. In case the district body is not able to meet by or before 31st December, the annual MGNREGA plan for the next year is deemed to be approved. The problem with the implementation of the scheme in the state is also with the shortage of adequate staff and adhoc nature of staffing such as Programme Officers have been appointed on contractual basis with no financial or drawing and disbursing powers.

Issues and Challenges in Implementation of MGNREGS in J&K

1. Administrative and Institutional Challenges: MGNREGA implementation deeply relies on the 73rd constitutional amendment which envisages a strong role for panchayat institutions in the states for local governance. However, in J&K panchayat institutions are governed by J&K Panchayat Raj Act 1989 which does incorporate a three-tier institutional system but it doesn't guarantee the same level of powers to these institutions *(Mushtaq Ahmad, 2014)*.

In J&K state, MGNREGA was implemented in 2007 as Jammu & Kashmir Rural Employment Guarantee Scheme (JKREGS) due to states special constitutional position. With the formulation of the JKREGS, the State Employment Guarantee Council (SEGC) was also constituted in August 2007 *(Alam et al 2010)*. The panchayat institutions did not exist at the time of formulation of JKREGS in 2007 and that has lead to institutional vacuum till today in 2016.

The district development board (DDB) prepares annual plans for JKREGS which is normally done by Zilla Parishad in other states. These administrative and institutional dilemmas have adversely impacted the JKREGS effective implementation and outcomes in the state *(Mushtaq Ahmad, 2014)*.

2. Employment & Job Card Irregularities: The field survey in sample blocks revealed some major issues with the way MGNREGS is implemented in the study areas. The usual complaint reported was that right to 100 days guaranteed job exists only on papers and had no resemblance on the ground. In block Trehgam and Langate only few respondents stated that they have worked for 100 days in a year which is also supported by the official data. The same is true about other sample blocks of Poonch and Surankote.

The job cards are to be given once work is demanded by the households and relevant entries such as work and wage details are to be made appropriately. However, during the course of field visits in study area it was observed that various beneficiary households worked without job card and in some cases didn't knew anything about a Job Card. It was also stated by beneficiary households that wrong entries regarding wages and number of days worked were made and also the issue of bogus job cards was also reported by some respondents.

3. Wage & Work Related Issues: It was observed during field visits to sample blocks across Kupwara and Poonch that the issue of low wages coupled with delayed payments to beneficiary households was a major concern. The respondents reported that payment within 15 days as per guidelines was not followed on the ground. Besides, it was also reported by the officials that since minimum wages are very low compared to market wage rates that have compelled them to offer higher wages by consolidating various works and providing less than 100 days wage employment. This partially explains as to why beneficiary households reported less than 100 days work. However, the delayed wage payments as also supported by the official data on wages liability remains as the major roadblock as for as effective implementation and outcomes are concerned.

4. Work Contracts: The MGNREGA Act prohibits contracting various works as it aims to eliminate the system of middlemen for better delivery of benefits to the rural communities. However, it was observed during field discussions with villagers and other officials that work contracts are provided under the scheme to people who are close to higher ups and political parties. The wage component is then transferred to the accounts of bogus workers which are paid a small amount to maintain silence while the corrupt practice goes on. However, some field officials reported inability in engaging people at meager wage rate in the scheme which forces them to engage in works contracting in the scheme.

5. No Social Audit: - The MGNREGA Act provides for social audit to be held after every six months but in the study area no social audit was held & even majority of the people were not aware of social audit. This is a major challenge for implementing agencies to ensure that the regular audits are conducted as the positive impact of the scheme is heavily dependent on the accountability of implementing agencies through the instrument of social audit. The issue of bogus accounts and bogus job cards and wrong entries thereof can be explained by the absence of social audits in the study area as it is a vital mechanism for ensuring effective implementation of MGNREGS in the study area as well as in the entire state of J&K.

Table 33: Social Audit in The Study Area

Social Audit	Frequency	Percent
NEVER	79	39.5
RARELY	97	48.5
SOMETIMES	23	11.5
FREQUENTLY	1	.5
Total	200	100

Source: Field Survey

The data in table 4.3 shows the response of participants and rural households on social audit in works selection and execution in the scheme. The results show that around 40% respondents reported that social audit has never been conducted on various works in the scheme and only one respondent reported positively on the social audit. This clearly reflects on the inefficiency and incompetence of implementing machinery and lack of social audit defeats the basic purpose of decentralized structure of the scheme.

Figure 6: Graphic Representation of Social Audit Data

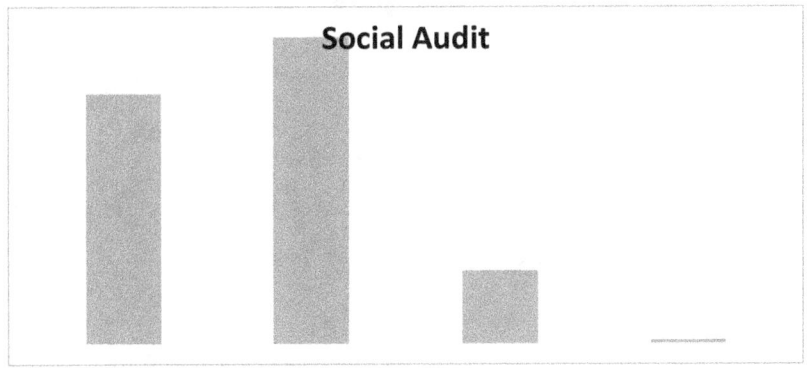

1=Never, 2=Rarely, 3=Sometimes, 4=Frequently

5. Geographic, Seasonal and Political Challenges: The effective implementation of MGNREGS is also hampered by the geographic and more so by the seasonal and political disturbances. The sample districts of Poonch and Kupwara are located on a hilly terrain and experience harsh weather conditions for more than 5 to 6 months in a year which badly affects the assets creation and meeting the right to 100 days wage employment guarantee under the Act. The issue of political disturbances has also from time to time impeded the overall development of the state in general and border areas in particular. For instance, the good part of FY 2008, 2010 and 2016 and coupled with the massive floods of FY 2013 has badly damaged the infrastructure in the state. Therefore, geo-political challenges also hamper effective implementation of the scheme in the state.